Winner of the L. E. Phillabaum Poetry Award for 2009

D1304351

Also by Daniel Hoffman

POETRY

Makes You Stop and Think: Sonnets
Beyond Silence: Selected Shorter Poems, 1948–2003
Darkening Water
Middens of the Tribe
Hang-Gliding from Helicon
Brotherly Love
The Center of Attention
Striking the Stones
Broken Laws
The City of Satisfactions
A Little Geste
An Armada of Thirty Whales

TRANSLATION

A Play of Mirrors, poems by Ruth Domino

PROSE

Zone of the Interior: A Memoir, 1942–1947
Words to Create a World
Faulkner's Country Matters
Barbarous Knowledge: Myth in the Poetry of Yeats, Graves, and Muir
Poe Poe Poe Poe Poe Poe Poe
Form and Fable in American Fiction
The Poetry of Stephen Crane
Paul Bunyan, Last of the Frontier Demigods

AS EDITOR

Over the Summer Water, poems by Elizabeth McFarland
Ezra Pound and William Carlos Williams
Harvard Guide to Contemporary American Writing
American Poetry and Poetics
The Red Badge of Courage and Other Tales

the
whole
nine yards

LONGER POEMS

Daniel Hoffman

LOUISIANA STATE UNIVERSITY PRESS
BATON ROUGE

NATIONAL
ENDOWMENT
FOR THE ARTS

*This publication is supported in part by an award
from the National Endowment for the Arts.*

Published by Louisiana State University Press
Manufactured in the United States of America
First printing

DESIGNER: Michelle A. Neustrom
TYPEFACE: Bembo
PRINTER AND BINDER: Thomson-Shore, Inc.

LIBRARY OF CONGRESS CATALOGING-IN-PUBLICATION DATA

Hoffman, Daniel, 1923–
    The whole nine yards : longer poems, new and selected / Daniel Hoffman.
    p. cm.
    ISBN 978-0-8071-3413-9 (cloth : alk. paper) — ISBN 978-0-8071-3414-6 (pbk. : alk. paper)
    I. Title.
    PS3515.O2416W47 2009
    811'.54—dc22

                                                                    2008042282

contents

THIS BOOK presents tales and suites exploring violence and transcendence, and comprises my third volume of selected poems, following *Beyond Silence: Shorter Poems, 1948–2003* and *Makes You Stop and Think: Sonnets* (2005). The six narratives here were too long and disparate in subject for inclusion in my collections of shorter poems. The suites are groups of poems that cling together and are reprinted from books of mine long out of print.

My hope in writing these longer poems has been to make them as different from one another as I can, and to share with readers the pleasures of exploring resources of language, theme, and form not attempted elsewhere in my work.

THE WHOLE NINE YARDS

BUDDIES

Passing their hotel on my lonely way
To a movie, I had to envy all the fun,
The comradeship of men acting like kids
Though more than twice my age—the Legionnaires
Fanned out and took over, swaying arm in arm,
Interrupting their own hoarse renditions
Of "Over There" to make unmannerly proposals
To clerk-typists heading to the subway.
Some, still in the hotel, leered from windows
And there'd be a flat, pop-off sound
As a water-bag from the tenth floor hit the pavement
Splashing passers-by and the jalopy
Crammed with conventioneers on which they'd painted
"40 & 8" and driven it on the sidewalk.
Only a week before I'd seen, outside a junkshop
In a bookbin, *A Pictorial History of the A.E.F.*
For a dime—who'd give a dime for the A.E.F.
When Okies, and the Lindbergh baby,
And transatlantic travel by dirigible
From Berlin to Lakehurst in two days
Were on everybody's mind? That afternoon
I may have been the only person in all
48 states who pored over the brownish photographs
Of hayseed boys lined up beneath a flagpole
Somewhere in Indiana, the felt hats
At jaunty angles, a gang of Penrod's friends.
On the next page they're marching eagerly
Toward a mess hall. Then the regiment
In parade formation behind massed flags
On Governor's Island, with the Woolworth Building
Piercing the sky behind them, and turn the page
To see them singing their way up the gangplank

Of the liner with four stacks and tiger-
Stripes of camouflage. France is not
Indiana—the villages a litter
Of burned houses, broken walls, horses
On their backs in the empty square, bellies
Bloated and legs stuck in the sky, the sky
A pyre of smudges raked by splintered trees.
"Fun in the Trenches" shows Our Boys at poker,
Crouched like ants within their sandbag tunnel
Till "The Attack" and creeping on their elbows
Between the craters, cannonade bursting
Here, and here, and see, some are hit
Are bleeding, others try to run, but run
Into barbed wire, strung out on the wire
Like scarecrows, sagging in their ripped cloth coats
In silhouette against the shrapnel glare
But here, here are those who made it, though wounded,
Loaded like cordwood in the ambulance.
Next page, recuperation at base hospital—
A file of boys with the same unthinking smiles
As at enlistment, lined up for the group picture—
Leaning on crutches, each has lost a leg;
On the bench, their trousers tucked around their stumps,
A row of legless men, and a nurse, standing.
They can smile—the next one can't, because—
Oh, the back of his neck curves in a sensuous way,
Comely is the profiled ear, the forehead
High and noble, but from there on
There's nothing you could describe, except the eye,
Large and moist, but no cheekbone,
No nose, no jaw, a sort of purse
Of skin gathered into a single aperture
Through which breath, a straw for drink or such could enter
But certainly no speech can come. Doctors
Have done their best for him. How does he live?

In a room with no mirrors. Of what can he think?
He will be lucky if he's spared remembering.
Lucky if his hands are gone so he can't touch
Where his face was. Is there a nurse who cares for him
—I mean, as a woman for a man? Further
Pages of boys with unmarked faces riding
On lorries decked with flowers and in boxcars
Painted "40 & 8" returning to the P.O.E.
And troopships coming home to crowds, more tributes
Of flowers, confetti, mustering-out parades
Before I was even born, and here, the buddies,
40-year-olds, are on a toot, certainly
Not recollecting barbed wire. It couldn't
Have been the soldier with no face, up there
In the Hotel Astor, who dropped the bag of water
That landed like a gun going off and splattered
The newsboy's brandished extras with their bold
Headlines, something about Sudetenland.

Penrod: Hero of Booth Tarkington's boys' book, popular in the
1920s and '30s.
40 & 8: Capacity of French boxcars: eight horses or forty men.
P.O.E.: Port of Embarkation.
Sudetenland: Province of Czechoslovakia seized by the Nazis,
October 15, 1938, after the Munich Agreement assured Hitler of no
retaliation from Britain or France. This aggression inevitably led a
year later to the Second World War.

THE LOVE CHILD

He was my bunkmate in the barracks and, like me,
Had nowhere else to go come Christmas, neither
Folks nor home. That made a brotherhood
Between us, as though orphans shared a bond
Of blood, or something close to blood. We flew
AT-6 trainers, sleek though slow.
When fitted with machine guns, half the two-bit
Armies in South America used them for fighters.
You could half-pretend you're slicing sky
In a P-47C like these, though these
Are twice the size, at least three times as fast.
My buddy lost one—an AT-6, that is,
But didn't tell me how, not then, nor after
Two months in the hospital he rejoined us.
It wasn't until the night before we flew
Our first mission across the Channel, as though
He couldn't bear to keep it all inside him
Knowing he might never have another
Chance to tell.
                    Wing-man in a "V"
From Albany to Loring A.F.B.
When in a sudden storm above the mountains
He lost his leader and the other wing.
Lightning like strobe-lights all around him—
Huge surges, electric system dead—
No compass, no altimeter, no radio,
Dead to rights in downdraft plunging,
Jerked back the stick to climb, and smashed
Into the mountain, his wings sheared off. A jolt
Threw his head against the panel—Flash!
A spurt of fire—as flame licked and leaped
Across the cockpit, drops of gas turned orange

On the windshield, heat pulsed through him,
Must have been by instinct that he thrust
The cockpit open, and jumped clear
Of the burning plane, jumped through a wall of fire
Into a bank of snow.
                              It was the snow
He sank way down in that protected him,
Kept him from being fried to cinders, kept
Him from passing out. Somehow, he struggled
Out of the snowbank, staggered down the rocks,
Found at last a cowpath or a trail,
Gaps between the boulders and stone fences
All glazed with ice or mounded under snow
Until, he had no way to tell how long,
How far he'd come, he came to someone's farmhouse,
A single light in a window heaped with snow.

    All right, he stumbled, feet half frozen, hands
Numb, he knocked, knocked on the splintered door.
Knocked again. No answer. Now he called,
"Hey in there! Help! Let me in! Help! Help!"
At last the door swung open just a crack,
A crack, no more, the door fast on a chain.
He could see it was a woman. She
Could see he was a stranger in the storm,
Snow swirling round him, heaping on his head,
And who'd expect a caller in a blizzard?
"Help!" he pleaded, "I'm an Air Force pilot,
Crashed my plane up there . . ." and slumped, exhausted
On her sill. At that she must have figured
It was safe to let the poor guy in
To thaw before he froze fast to her doorsill.
Not till he was inside and got his eyes
Used to the low gleam of one kerosene
Lantern did he see her, maybe forty,
Fifty, hard to tell, so beaten down

By hard living, although her face still showed
It had been pretty once, or beautiful.
But now, wrapped in an old shawl with her hair
Hanging straight, her hands gnarled, leaning
On a crutch, on a crumpled, twisted leg,
She was gazing at him with intensity
So odd, so keen, he didn't know what to say.
She spoke: "I knew that you'd return some day.
I knew you would come home." "Come home?
I don't know where I am, I've lost my plane
In a blizzard on your mountain—I don't know
What *state* we're in—I've never been so lost,
Never been here before." But she bent down,
Put some more sticks on the hearth,
Then, as the flames lit up the room, she said,
"I knew you'd find your way to me somehow,
No matter what they did to you, or me . . ."
By now he couldn't help but think that this
Is what can come of living all alone
In a smoky farmhouse halfway up a mountain,
A poor lame woman who has lost her wits.
"No matter what they did or where they'd send you,
I knew you'd find me," as she set before him
Cold biscuits and a pot of lukewarm tea,
And, limping, pushed another chair to the table
And sat across from him, the smoking lamp
Casting her shadow huge against the wall.
She poured, in two chipped cups, and then,
As though she'd held it in for years, for years
No one to tell it too, a flood of words
Spilled out—She'd never had but one, the one
Man she'd loved, her father's hired man.
How handsome he was, how strong, who'd come one summer
From nobody knew just where, no family,
Owned nothing but the clothes he wore, but worked

Long, worked hard, and took meals at this table
And slept on a cot in the barn. Even her father,
A hard, cold man, admitted, "He's a good one"
—How good her father couldn't know. "I'd meet him
In the barn—if father wasn't looking,
At first he'd smile at me, and then he'd say
Some little things none of the louts near here
Had ever said or could have thought. If I smiled,
He'd say his morning was a field of daisies,
But if I frowned his day would never thaw.
Sweet nothings, people call them, but people here
Had no use for nothings, except me.
From smiles he went to touches, and his touch
Upon my arm set tingles in my blood,
I'd feel the color rising, and he'd steal
His arm around me, pull me close, then drop it,
Turn, and reach his hoe down from the wall
Just as my father blocked the sunlit door—
I hadn't heard him coming, for the beating
Of the pulse within my head. Father, with work
And only work upon his mind, would notice
Nothing, but Mother, though she'd married Father,
Could see that for the first time in my life
I was happy, and she figured why.
When she told Father what she'd figured, he
Didn't stop to ask, but on the minute
Paid him off and fired him and forbade
He'd ever come back to our farm. He walked
Whistling down our lane, with Father muttering
Threats, Mother grimly silent, and I,
I wept and sobbed, eyes streaming at my chores.
That night, though, in the blackest darkness
I heard a sound, a whistle at my window.
And there he'd leaned against my sill the ladder
Father'd left down after mending gutters.

'Come on,' he whispered, 'we'll get out of here,'
And I threw down some clothes and climbed across
The sill. I felt his hands steady the ladder,
Then their window-sash flung open, and Mother
Crying a curse on him spawned beneath
A bush who'd steal their daughter, a man so foul
They'd not have him break bread at their table,
And Father called him a bastard fiend while I
Tried to slide the rungs and dash into the woods
With him—they called me Strumpet! Fool! Whore
Of Babylon! I screamed, 'Leave us alone!
You'll never see us—' but the night roared
With a flash from the window and single moan
On the ground below. 'You've killed him!' I sobbed
And jumped to be beside him in the blackness,
Leaped not seeing where the ground was, landed
With my leg twisted beneath me
Broken, and me holding his head bleeding
In my arms, bleeding.
                    "Father carried me
Into the parlor, laid me on the divan,
Then dragged him out into the pasture where
He dug the grave. He'd never tell me where.
I lay there in the parlor with my leg
Knitting wrong—no doctor in the village,
Not that they'd have called one if there were,
For none should know the murder or their shame,
Nor doctor eight months later when I gave
Birth to his baby son. My parents spoke
No word to me from that night on, and when
I could limp about with a stick and do my chores
I did them till my time came, never hearing
One word spoke to me. But my baby,
My baby cooed and cried and gurgled, all
To me, to me, for he was mine. But they,

They took him from me, wrested from my arms
My baby, Father whipping the horse, my baby
In a basket next him on the wagon seat,
As I tried to hobble after them
Falling on stones, my mother grimly watching
All the while. From that day on I never
Said one word to them. This house heard
No words. No words
When Father sickened, lay face to the wall,
No words when he died. No words when Mother
And I dragged his body to the orchard
And together, silent, dug his grave.
No words for years, then, as we moved about
This house, and all the while I waited here
Knowing wherever he had placed my baby,
Whatever orphanage, or family, or town,
My boy would someday come."

                                    All this time
He sat there unbelieving while her story
Poured from her, yet felt a strange tingling
Sense of dread, for he had never known
Who were his real parents, or his name.
"Come, my son," she pulled herself and him,
Grasped his hand, tugged him from the chair
Took the lamp and lurched him toward the stairs,
Then, on the dusty landing, leaned against a door.
The lamplight caught a thousand dustmotes, spreading
Gleams across the floor. There, in a chair,
A woman sat, an old, old woman, chained
By one foot to the chair. "Here is my son,
My child you stole from me, you murderers,
You killed his father and stole my child, Mother,
I've waited twenty years to show you him,
Twenty years to tell him what you'd done,
And how does it please you now to be the one

Imprisoned? Hah, she has no answer, has
No words," and with a laugh lurched near the chair.
Then he could see what sat in it was dead,
In a dress a corpse, head shriveled like a mummy's,
Mummy hands. With the lamp she trembled so,
Trembled, stumbled, twisted leg went crumpled,
Fell sprawled against the chair, let fall
The lamp. The corpse fell off, fell in a cloud
Of dust in pieces on the floor, the scene
Suddenly brilliant as spilled kerosene
Caught fire and flames now leapt around the room,
Flames licking dried-out dress, the rushes
On the chair seat, flecks of flame like fireflies
As the dust caught fire, the crackling curtains,
The woman screaming in the midst of flames,
And he again beating at flames, beating
His hands against the huge hot surges burning
His skin, his hair, hearing her screams, her whimpers,
The whole room now a mass of orange tongues
He tried to reach her through them, they were beating
Upon him, scorched his eyes, his breath, he couldn't
Breathe, he staggered to the landing, flames
Pursuing him, the whole house crackling, back
To where he saw a dark square. There he jumped
Through glass, the snow all orange below him
As the house blazed up into the storm, the sky,
And fell deep in a snowbank. Melting snow
Protected him from being burned alive.
Somehow staggered to his feet, he guessed
A good while later, for behind him a smoking
Mass of embers, not a house, in snow
Stumbling through snowfall down the icy rocks
Until he found a cowpath or a trail
Among the gaps between the stones and boulders
Or trees and snowmounds where the boulders were.

The sky was lighter now, the snow stopped falling,
A wind came up and whipped him with loose snow
Until—he had no way to tell how long,
How far he'd come—he came to someone's farmhouse,
Light in a window, and slumped against their door.
They sledged him down the mountain to the village,
Called the State Police, who fetched him out
To the Army hospital. Two months
Till he recovered, then joined us here, in England.
He never knew the family's name—no chance
To backtrack up the mountain to that farmhouse
Where they took him in and ask the folks
Who were they that farmed high up the mountain,
Where there was a woman with a twisted leg?
When he was well enough they shipped him here,
But when this war is over, he'll go back
To Maine and find that mountain, evidence
Of fires and a wrecked plane deep in the woods—he will,
If we return from where we're bound today,
Wherever it is—the C.O. wouldn't say—
They've loaded ammo and filled our tanks for.
Thumbs up—you be here when I taxi home!

A BARN BUILT IN OHIO

All I asked for was the way to Dayton.
If you've lost the way to where you're going,
Chances are you don't know where you've been,
He said, in coveralls as faded blue
As the tattered billboard on the barn behind him.
I, in city duds, made out *Gillette*.
You've heard, he asked, knowing I had not,
Of Cedarville, which you are in? We're famed
For the world's biggest barn, here, in Ohio.
I didn't know, I said.—It's not three miles
From here to my Great Grand Uncle's farm. He'd come
To Xenia to sell his calves at the County Fair
And drive his two-year-old in the sulky race.
You take a proud man and a speedy horse
He's raised up from a colt, oh you can bet
His friends put up a stake he'd run to win.
That year there came the biggest crowd that ever
Flocked to Xenia—why, thousands swarmed to see
A real live Russian race his great black mare.
That horse was huge. Her nostrils' snorts were thunder.
Her great black forelegs flashed, the sulky swished
Past the grandstand, wheels a whizzing blur.
They all said there's just no touching her.
And nobody'd ever seen a real live Russian
In Green County, with his great tall hat
Of fur, a beard of briars, a riding coat
With five rows of buttons big as dollars
And an ebony-handled whiplash six yards long.
If you looked toward his boot-toes you would see
Twice reflected upwards from his toe-points
Your own face gaping at you, weasel-small.
The race? They ran the race twice over—

Had to, for the first they ran dead heat,
The second, nose to nose, an even draw.

    The folks 'round here, they would have liked to win
But they were civil to him just the same.
And then he started in about his *barn*
—Not his, exactly, but the barn he'd raised
His horses in, somewhere out there by Moscow.
Belonged, he said, to the Czar of all the Russians.
What they couldn't stand was hearing him
After our colt had all but beat his mare
Talk up his biggest, tallest, cleanest barn,
So large a troop of cavalry could drill in it,
So tall that when the trumpeters would blow
They had to wait ten minutes for the echo,
So clean they fed the horses in a pasture
While the Czar's wife and her ladies dined inside.

    This Uncle I was telling you about
Burned to hear it. Lies, a pack of lies,
He thought, but who could prove those lies were lies?
Only thing to do then was disprove them.
He asked the Russian for the measurements,
He thanked the Russian for the plan,
Inviting him to call out at his farm
Next year, if he should care to race again,
Then rode directly back to Cedarville
And sold three lots, a pasture and a pond.
The snow was deep in drifts that winter,
Not much travel then through Cedarville
But one or two who sleighed it brought reports
Of crackling pine trees falling in a forest,
The crunch of trunk and tearing of the boughs,
Sudden silence under wheeling crows,
Zip-zip of bucksaw, snap of hammer

Reverberating in the icy air.
Come Spring, some waggoners came in from Springfield
Bearing tales of something in the woods—
Great posts standing far apart as chimneys.
Next, some told of crosspieces laid down
And there's a great gazebo in a clearing,
A god-sized arbor waiting for the grape
Though Uncle's cornfields were pecked bare by crows
And the clapboards on his house now needed paint.
Even his kitchen-garden ran to weeds,
But then we heard of twelve-inch boards and roofing
Being nailed up on the bony scaffolding.
They said it was the largest, tallest octagon
—A beauty—ever seen. He took the measure
From the Russian's yarn about that royal barn and added
American timber, two yards to each dimension.
The top where all eight angles came together
Wore a windowed skylight like a crown.
Inside, the sunlight tumbled through and silvered
Everything it touched by day with moonlight.
Inside it was so big that when his baby
Son crawled through the front door, he attained
Majority by the time he reached the back.
So tall it was in the cupola, the birds
That nested never touched the ground: they laid
Eggs on the second highest tier of rafters,
Those hatching there came down two tiers and laid
Again, and their eggs, hatching, hopped to the floor.
That floor was where the 31st Ohio
Regiment of Horse practiced its famous charge.
Yet it was clean—so clean that when the Regiment
Went to the War, the floor smelt meadow-sweet
With not a whiffle of horse-sweat or man-sweat.

You'd like to see that barn? You would have thought
Driving through Cedarville, you'd find it yet—
You came that way and didn't see it?
If it was there I guess you would have seen it.
I was shown it once by the son of the man
Who's son of the man who entered through one door
A babe, and emerged to vote for Garfield. Pa
Pointed out to me the birds that flew
To nests in crossbeams only part-way down.
(His father was Lieutenant in the Regiment
that mustered out by moonlight there.) But he
Who made the best-barned county in the world right here
Although the shutters banged about his house,
Waited, while termites gnawed the pillars of his porch;
Waited, while his neglected fields were ploughed by moles;
Waited, while his sons left home—what could they do at
    home?—
And thistles broke the ground his poor wife sleeps in;
He waited, for a visitor who never came
To admire his barn or race in the Xenia Fair.
Somebody saw a piece in the paper saying
The Russians no longer raced in sulky races—
Showed a picture of their Czar's big barn
—I must admit that Russian barn was big,
Though not, of course, a patch on Uncle's barn.
Long since his horses have been let to pasture
Or the glue works. Horses everywhere
Grew few while tractors rutted in the cornfields.
Meantime his boards dried out, the shingles split,
Rain in the wind and snow seeped in, the walls
Swayed in the cold night wind, beams creaked and groaned.
Across the drill floor sumach and redbud marched
A second growth of saplings pierced the rooftree.
It fell in the center of the hundred houses
You drove through just before you took this fork.

Now if you take this road, halfway to Dayton
Through the chain-link fence you'll get a glimpse
Of a silo and a hangar by the runway.
You've never seen a runway near so long—
The red and green and yellow lights that line it
Stretch and disappear in Indiana.
That hangar is the broadest, tallest hangar
Ever set beside a runway: doors
Are seven storeys tall, and what's so tall
It takes a seven-storey door to hide it?
Whatever it is, it's taller than the silo.
Whatever's hidden in the silo, bulking
One-third the way into the steely sky
But sunk deep down below the topsoil covered
With the runway's blacktop and parade of lights.
Deep in its concrete bed it lies, awaiting
A signal to begin the race, or end it.
But there's that fence to keep you at a distance.
Still, you can judge the scale. Well now, with chores
In the barn to do I can't spend all the forenoon
Gabbing with you, Mister. Dayton's *this* way.

SHOCKS

Trouble with the brakes? I'll have a look
soon as I've put these new shocks
on Wendell's pickup. You know Wendell,
drives around—or used to—in that orange Maverick
with the .30-.30 looking like a cannon
on the rear windshield shelf. You wouldn't want
to mess around with him. When they had boxing
Friday nights in Ellsworth, he
clobbered the piss out of three
midshipmen from the Maritime—

Each week they had to stop the bout.

That was Fridays. Saturdays, watch out!
When Wendell got lit up
you wouldn't want to mess with him.
Even when he worked he was a wild one—
in the woods, he'd lean on his McCulloch
like he had a grudge against the trees.
We knew we had a bad egg there,
and it's for sure that if our Deputy
had had the balls to take him in,
Wendell would have ate Thanksgiving turkey
more than once behind the wall at Thomaston.
But then damned if he didn't straighten out, work hard, save his
    money, buy this pickup, an old flat-bed truck, take a loan on a
    backhoe and pay off his Maverick.

You must have seen that orange Maverick.
Will you hand me that wrench there?
Next he bought himself a mobile home.
Set it on an acre on the Kerry Road

back in the woods beyond the blueberries.
Makes you wonder what Jeanette imagined,
her being such a pretty little girl,
she could make of that big brawler just by marrying him.
One month she's jumping around the high school gym
—"*GIVE US AN E! GIVE US AN A!*"—for the Eagles—
waving pompoms in her tight white sweater,
and next you know she's married, moving
in that trailer in the woods with Wendell,
with Wendell gone all day.
It's been two years. Since then
no man in town's worked hard as Wendell
cutting wood, clearing land, ploughing
fields in summer, roads and driveways in the snow,
hauling rock, whatever's to be done. And then
he got that backhoe.
He'll clear a woodlot of stumps to make a pasture,
that bucket jammed among the roots of big old spruces
at just the angle
to break the whole stump free.

You ever seen that sewer line along State Road?

He has a touch with that machine so fine
you'd think he's bringing in a trout hooked on his lure.

And after a day's work, in the hour or two
between supper and the dark
he drives that Maverick with Jeanette beside him,
and his foot on the floor—

When I'm slipping the padlock through the hasp
there's a scream of rubber yelping 'round the curve,
a smear of orange
—it's Wendell and Jeanette

tear-assing toward Blue Hill.
Where did I put those pliers?

One afternoon last week when he came home
no supper's on the stove,
and Jeanette's sobbing like a broken heart.

She'd had a visit
from the tax man.

In the middle of the forenoon, when any fool should know
Wendell wouldn't be at home.
Where's he gonna be but out at work
earning his pay so Uncle Sam can tax him?
Jeanette, she says her husband isn't home.
Taxman says. That don't matter,
—you're just as liable as he is,
so I'll take the matter up with you.
And she's so young, so trusting,
she opens the trailer door and lets him in.

He crosses out
damned near everything on Wendell's Schedule C,
business expenses: So many bucks for gas,
depreciation, so much for repairs.
Because Jeanette can't show receipts.
You know, he says, it says here in these tax instructions
taxpayer responsible for keeping records.
But Wendell, he don't keep no records.
He pays cash for everything,
Every tank of gas, each tire, each set of points or plugs.
I write the bill up every time—

he crumples up receipts to light his stove.

Without receipts you got no more chance against the
    government
than a mackerel in a herring weir.

Those damned fools in Bangor, what do they believe
a taxpayer like Wendell pours
into the fuel tank of his pickup,
chainsaw, flatbed, backhoe, and his Maverick—
free jugs of percolated porpoise-piss?—
they sure as hell don't let him charge
a nickel off for gas.
So what with this and that he ends up owing
the Government of the United States
for the past three years a total of back taxes
and interest on the taxes, and penalties
for not paying the interest and the taxes
he didn't know he owed,
it come to damn near *two thousand bucks.*

Now where in hell's hot oven is Wendell
gonna get two thousand bucks?
So taxman looks around the yard.
There's the old flatbed, dented like a dead beer can.
There's the backhoe—what's the government want with a used
    backhoe?
Yeah, but look—there's last year's Maverick,
bright as half a unsucked orange, with only
12,000 miles, just sitting there.
So he fills out a lien on the Maverick
in full payment of all back taxes and interest and penalties due
    thereunto
and hands it to Jeanette.
then climbs back in his long black LTD
and tools on home to the office in Bangor.

Ever seen one of them taxmen?
Pasty-faced fellows, come from sitting under a fluorescent light in
    the office all day, same kind of light
they put in a chicken house. Face
the color of mushroom.
Thin around the shoulders, too,

They don't get no healthful exercise to build the body
except they sharpen a pencil.

Well, Wendell looks at the form.
He reads it real close, and then
he tells Jeanette to never mind,
let's take us one last drive before we turn it in.
That night I never *seen* them coming round this curve,
I heard that orange rocketship blast off
already past me half a mile down the road
doing 90!

Next day he didn't go to work till late
—used my phone here, so I heard him say
he couldn't take the time from work
to bring the car in during hours.
O.K. then if he brings it in at night,
to the Municipal Parking Lot? Sure,
he'll leave the key and title. Then he says,
real nice like, Yes sir, they will be
under the seat. On the driver's side.

That evening him and Jeanette had some beers together.
Then he took the maul he splits his wood with
and stove in both the headlights and the turning lights.
Then he climbed up in the backhoe, drove it over
right longside the car,

set down the stilts, then lifted up the bucket.
Down he brings the bucket—

and the hood's smashed
like a birdcage that a horse just stepped on.
The bucket swings up high, then down
he brings the bucket
and the roof crumples
like Mount Katahdin slid on it.
Then he leans two planks against the flatbed's tail
and buckets that miserable wreck
until he's got it nudged onto the truck.

In the middle of the night, in Bangor,
in the Municipal Parking Lot
he pushed his orange Maverick overboard,
climbs down, unsheathes his hunting knife and jabs it deep
into the rims of all four tires and the spare.

Didn't get back to the trailer till nearly daylight.

That day he came by in the pickup
And used my phone again.
Did you find my Maverick, he says.
Good. Did you find the keys?
That's good. The title?
That's good too. It's all yours . . .
Now mister,
shut your trap and you hear me.
Your goddam form that requisitioned
my car didn't specify
in what condition

the car was to be turned in. So you have got it
in the condition it is in.

And one thing more,
Mister, if you ever come to the Kerry Road
when I ain't home and you
knock on my door again
and trouble my wife again,
I'll tail you back to Bangor, mister,
I'll stash your ribs in like a pile
of matchstick kindling,
I'll bash your face
till your own mother could mistake it
for a pail of squid cut up for lobsterbait.
Do you get me, mister?

I would say, Wendell made himself
sufficiently clear. The man,
he assured him right away,
his tax case is settled and closed.

It does a fellow good to get some satisfaction.

JANE DOE

Who can say why a person would want
To shove a shopping-bag into the trash
In the women's room of the restaurant
(The Howard Johnson called "The James Fenimore Cooper")

On the Jersey Turnpike? "From the trash I heard
A faint sound, like some little creature
Rustling its paper nest with a whimper.
Of course I was scared,"

The woman told her story
Who luckily just then was cleaning the lavatory
(To be sure she wasn't cleaning at all
While smoking a butt with the *Daily News* in a stall)—

She thought it was maybe a mouse or a rat
Had got into the trash can,
Though it didn't make sense, she said, to imagine that
Since she keeps the Ladies' as clean as she can.

A little afeared, she reached among crumpled papers.
Towels, Kleenex, wrappers and diapers
Till she grabbed the handles of a shopping bag.
Maybe, she thought, there's a kitten inside the bag?

She pulled it out and opened it up and saw
And screamed "My God! A baby!" In less than a minute
Waitresses, customers, cooks, busboys, men
All crowded the washroom. Somebody phoned the Law

And the radio car squealed into the lot. The trooper
Leaps out with his pencil and forms.
Now you know if it had been a boy
They'd have named him James Fenimore Cooper

But he writes down instead, "Name: Jane Doe,
Sex: F. Age: About 2 hrs. Race:
White?" and from his dashboard radio
Calls in an urgent message for all cars to trace

The mother, the parents, request they come forth, repeat
Come forth—Parents, it's been three days now,
Your daughter still lacks your name,
You can have the baby without the blame—

The media will soon tire of seeking you.
But don't you watch TV? Haven't you seen her photo
In the *Daily News*? It looks like no
Human birth can be acknowledged for Baby Doe.—

Say, don't you hunger for your child? You're on a beach
In Florida by now, or you've reached Chicago
Or you're eating sundaes in another HoJo?
Maybe you are not with each

Other any more. Baby Jane Doe's mother
Maybe hasn't laid her eyes on the father
Since a certain night last summer . . .
Ms. Doe, where are you with your belly

Flat at last but slack and flabby
And a heaviness in your empty womb?
Where are you with your leaky breasts and no
Toothless mouth to guzzle and nurse at them?

Somewhere, behind locked doors in a rented room
Your hormones are in an uproar. You try forgetting
But that won't work. So you try not thinking.
But that won't work. You'll have to learn

To live without what's missing. Dull heat
Seethes in your bowels like acid etching
The outlines of an unseen portrait.
The face that trembles beneath your trembling hands

Shows the world's a little colder, older.
Little mother, little mother,
Where is your summer evening's paramour?
Where is Mr. Richard Roe?

Laying patches with his souped-up Chevrolet,
He's hanging round a Burger King for meat,
Chatting up a waitress for a lay.
Once he's got her splayed on the back seat

And she's sliding her pantyhose back on
There's nothing to say, nothing between them. The stirred
And tickled tissues now subside. He's gone,
Leaving, in time, what he has spurred

Within her to be emitted in a parking lot,
Dropped like a cat's turd
And wrapped and thrown away. Had the cleaning woman
Not been stealing a smoke in the toilet just then,

Why, that particular bag of trash
Might have been thrust through the gaping door
Of the Municipal Garbage Incinerator
And a soul in an instant singed to ash

But instead was recycled, and Baby Jane
Given as much as three score and ten
Before dust turns to ashes and dust again,
Time for this babe in the arms of the State

To escape from her childhood's loveless cot
(Motherless, fatherless, she will recall
Intensely the smell of the starched white aprons
Worn by each of the matrons, the nursery matrons),

Time to grow taller, then plumper and fuller,
Time when her body is ripe to discover
For that love-stunted soul in her round yielding flesh
Whether the whole wide world can proffer

To her a true lover, time to fulfill
The mystery that is her destiny, to see if it will
Absolve the riddle of her setting forth
And redeem the misery of her birth.

SAMARITANS

Sunglints on wavelets, evanescent
glitter across baymouth, broken
by black humps rising, diving, heading
shoreward, inexorably shoreward. From the bluff
at Harborside with 8x50 Swiss binoculars
we could make out the shifting congregation
of black bumps where the water lightened near the reach,
huge tails flaying the air, hear
the *Splat!* a minute after seeing flukes
strike water, and people, small as ants
lining the shore, the lobster boats and outboards
circling out beyond the beached pod
of pilot whales. Everyone wants
to help them. Across the harbor we
are helpless, looking on, as
a fisherman in hipboots wades among the flashing
flukes—he holds a line, a cable,
look—he loops it over a tail, returns
to his craft, arms help him aboard, then puffs
of exhaust rise as they rev the engine
and the lobsterboat slowly, slowly chugs
into the channel hauling, tail-first, one
out toward open water. They've
cut him loose! A faint cheer, windwafted, floats
toward us. What now, though? Look,
the boat swerves shoreward once again—the whale
is heading back, is beached again. All
that work for nothing. There must be
thirty whales, at least, and the tide's
turning, flowing out beyond the islands, leaving
all those pilot whales there thrashing, higher

and higher on the beach.

The mass

suicides of whalels—why do they

do it? Every time a bulletin

flashes on the news—STRANDED WHALES

LINE SHORE—Smithsonian cetologists,

marine biologists, grant-funded animal

behaviorists, arriving after the deaths,

congregate on whale-littered shoals and shores,

postmortemizing, theorizing, giving

interviews. "SONAR FADEOUT

STRANDS WHALES," says Dutch zoologist W.

H. Dudek who accumulated records of 133 mass

strandings throughout the world. "Thousands

of whales . . . 29 different species . . . ,

generally stay in deep water." But two years later,

   "AUSTRALIAN SCOFFS

     AT WHALE SUICIDES

           —nothing

but an old wives' tale in the view of W.

H. Dawbin, whale biologist at University of

Sydney. "'The reasons are unknown,'

he said, 'but they could be

accidental.'" And then,

   "200 WHALES DIE IN FLORIDA

     AFTER MASS SWIM TO BEACHES

—'They seem determined

to do away with themselves,' St. Lucie County

Administrator Weldon Lewis said today . . .

At the water's edge near Fort Pierce

mass burials were scheduled for whales

not washed back to sea . . . a disposal

rather than a rescue operation."

Another several years with no beachings,

then,

"SCIENTISTS STUDY MYSTERY

OF 24 PILOT WHALES THAT DIED

AFTER STRANDING ON CAROLINA BEACH

—After ten days, autopsies indicated
parasites in the inner ear had adversely
affected their sense of direction." A theory
gaining wide acceptance until, after six years,
"A Mexican scientist believes he has determined
why 56 sperm whales swam ashore to their deaths
on the coast of Baja California. . . . 'Because
of the outgoing tide in the channel they
panicked.'" All 41 sperm whales beached
near Florence, Oregon that June
died, and biologists from Oregon State analyzed
tissue samples to search for disease. "'It's
real sad,' said Diane Blundell of Eugene
who went to the beach with buckets
to help pour water on the whales. 'If I
could pick them up and carry them out,
I would.'" A year after that

"IO LARGE SPERM WHALES DIE

AFTER ENTERING SHALLOW INLET

—Preliminary studies of whale carcasses revealed
no clear cause for the mass beaching in Camachee
Cove, Florida. Experts were puzzled."

In Australia
on shortwave, two whale-watchers hear
whales beached on the southern coast. This time
they're ready, tarps, ropes, buckets in their jeeps,
and helpers—vacationers and residents pour
onto the beach where the great beasts flounder,
wheeze, tails flapping, blowholes bubbling
as they gasp, the sand around them
drying in the sun. Bucket brigades

water the whales' skin while a team of twenty
slide tarps beneath the one still half in, half
out of the water. Gripping edges
of the tarp they gently ease him
down the beach until he floats, then gently,
gently, rock him back and forth from side to side
righting the sonar dislocation in
his inner ear. But when towed
outshore, and cast off, he, too, swims around,
then heads back toward the beach. All
that work for nothing? Again they ease him
on a tarp, then loop a line around his tail
and tow him out: this time he swims
in circles around the boat, then, at last,
heads toward the open sea. This,
repeated and repeated on each whale
still near enough to the water's edge to float.
One whale, sick, disoriented, had beached itself
and uttered whale-cries of distress (We
have heard their singing each to each,
we know they're social creatures, have
a language and respond). All the school
rallies to his aid. But they cannot
aid him. They too are beached, disoriented,
stranded by the outrush of the tide,
lungs crushed by their own weight, wheezing,
flukes more feebly flapping, gasping
while the remorseless sea
dries them and they die.
Trying to help them, we emulate
the whales.
    All men
are whalelike. A Chukchi hunter,
spear in mittened hand, plods the icebound
shore of Senyavin Strait, Siberia. One whale

would feed his family all winter. He rounds
a bend. The Strait is blocked, the East Wind drove
ice between Arakamchechen Island
and the shore. Sealed, solid with ice. He stands
astounded in the frigid wind: whales,
whales, whales, whales, hundreds of white
Beluga whales trapped
in the shrinking Strait, teeming
in the water, wheezing, shouldering each other.
The shoals of cod they chased are gone
beneath the ice, but whales must breathe the air
and cannot leave. His mukluks track
back to the village. Now headman
and fellow hunters retrace his trail.
"This is not good fortune. This is doom."
For if the whales cannot get out they all will die,
and the village, too, will perish.
On the trading-post shortwave the Stone Age
calls the Russian
Government: above Senyavin helicopters whirr,
verify report. Take photos, television film.
Settlers from Yanrakynnot fling frozen fish
into the water, to feed the swarming whales,
three thousand trapped there. What high command
decided that the icebreaker *Moskva,*
chaperoning freighters through the Bering floes,
instead should steam into Senyavin Strait
to free those whales? A spotter plane
to guide her, *Moskva* slowly batters
the ice, retreats, then throttles ahead
to crash again against the ice,
crumbling it, backing and forthing, cutting
a narrow channel through the glacial wall.
As the *Moskva* at last breaks through
Captain Kovalenko raises his cap, to the cheers

of all his crew, her bow among the whales
now weakened, starving, terrified
by this huge shuddering hull whose roars
they cannot understand.

                              To communicate
with whales, how can we tell them
what we mean, how tell them what we know?
First let the ship become familiar. Four days
she lies there among the whales, revving
her engines, shutting down; perhaps they'll learn
she does them no harm. Meantime the narrow
channel carved of ice begins to close.
By then the whales, fed now on air-dropped frozen
fish, accustomed to the *Moskva,* turn
sportive, dive and surface, blow and whistle, snort,
squeal, swim—but none makes for the channel. How
communicate with whales? It would take
an Orpheus to strum them into a trance, to charm—
Dolphins, one of the men remembers, respond
to music. So over the P.A. speakers on the deck
they try the *Moskva's* repertoire,
tapes of martial airs, "Rakoczi March," but overboard,
no response. Try something else:
balalaika tunes, choruses by the Folk Chorus
of the Caucasus Republic, the Peoples' Songs
of the Red Army Choir, Folk Minstrels
of Azerbejan—Belugas must belong
to a different republic. The sailors now have played
all their marches, folk songs, pop songs; one
last chance—the Captain has some tapes
of classics. Over the frosty air
the Moscow Symphony's timbres strike the water
—and now Belugas stop, and listen, and swarm
around the ship. She moves toward the channel slowy,
slowly, Belugas following the chords

that lace the air, she stops, then the propellers
whirl again and the whales follow, flukes
swirling in time to "Pictures at an Exhibition"
and to Chaliapin's arias from *Boris Godunof*
until the ship and all her whales reach,
at last, the freedom
of the open sea.

BLESSINGS

I

for Liz and Kate

1

When both our bodies in one whole
Were joined, their grubbing histories
& our lonely souls' imprisoned rant
Were swept immaterially aside
Unbearable exaltation shared
That throbbing unity of the sun
Until with death of boy & girl
Subsiding in the dark cocoon
Cradled in your curving thighs
And your head on my crooked arm
We were, unknowing, all we'd done,
As infants sleep before they're born.

2

Some instant in that deep fond sleep
Nor felt, recorded, now unknown,
A seed was sown.
Deep in your warm down body's weal
Two cells commingled: A soul leapt
From God's eye forth, alive & tingling,
And all that while
We slept.

3

Three months about our daily labours,
Buying groceries, reading the papers,
Beneath the navel now a bulge burgeons.

A face lies there with sunless features;
If plunged from the womb, a book advises
Into the terrifying brightness of the air

And placed then in a glass of water,
Would struggle feebly, simulating life,
This child not yet a child would surely die

Instinctively forfending death!
Three months about our daily labours:
Part way up the stairs, a pause for breath.

4

The year is half full swung now. We
Move more slowly than when last
Ripe apples pummelled the soft grass.

Who goes where we go? Who lives under
That anonymous mound? Our image
Through flickering centuries grows fuller

Past the pickerel, cygnet, hare,
Swims through sludge & stream & air
And wears the womb as atmosphere

And wears inviolable peace where there's no
Guilt nor knowledge and none's needed.
But your strength, your breath, your blood feed it.

5

Down green corridors of moan
Your voice tolled the spirit's pain.
Caught in the body's gripe, it wrung
Gnashes from that bravely muffled gong.
Your voice down greentiled aisles of pain
Piled agony upon my tight breast bone.

But you suffered alone.

What monstrous mechanism did I begin
That rams apart your wrenching bone?
What natural force makes the winds scream
And the seas swell
And star-clappers in the heavens toll?
I raised your clenched fist
And closed those nails about my wrist;
Hands that passion could transmit
Were powerless to couple pain.
Alone you bore birth's bruises.

Love puts our bodies to rude uses.

6

Nestle, darling on your mother's breast;
Let fade birth's roar and the first breath's shrill alarm,
Drink in her warm white sweetness, strength, and rest

Cradled in the crook of her curved arm.
Hush-a-bye, my crying tiny one,
I'll exorcise your sleep from hovering harm

And shade you from the pitiless mortal sun.
There is no going back to that dark place
Where life is effortless and pain was none.

Passion, time, and accident will trace
From the pealing clouds of this loud cockscrow's dawn
A destiny upon your cherished face,

While Father and Mother love you, and look on.

Fledgeformed nurseling, infinitely small
Yet fashioned cunningly and wholly dear,
None could foretell how we should more than all

Love love you, lying helpless here.
Our own lost infancies on your cries croon,
In you our childish lineaments reappear

More delicate, perfected at the bone.
One little needs imagine lithe girlgrace
As will attend your casual movements soon;

Blossoming from our lonely souls' embrace
Mindmagic, heartwish, will, will be your own.
Yet we're your lineage, you are all our race—

Three-personed, by continual love made one.

II

for MacFarlane

MYRTLE:

My gift is luck,
And when you've heard my charm you'll find
Little enough to do to him.
I sing,

> May no mischance befall you,
> No curse nor sickness gall you;
> From wind's cold lash and heart's despair
> These words I breathe into the air
> You breathe defend you:

> Now may your newborn spirit
> No grief, no dole inherit;
> May natural grace your graces feed,
> Fruition be your nurture's meed
> And joys attend you.

This boy's won luck and bounty. You can't harm him.

MORTA:

Very pretty. But here's a little song
To charm him:

> Sleep, little mannikin,
> Wrapt in your little skin.
> That sweeting soul that roundly snores
> Through that infant nose of yours
> Will someday wake, or dream, to know
> Its quickened image, nude Ego
> Wants all the world's glad rags for clothes;

Ambition's buttons fasten those
That choke contentment tight around
Your heart—the mortal cummerbund.
Nor wisdom stanch its inward itch
Which moral sense will, wretched, scratch.
These blessings come with your first teething.
Such joys you find are my bequeathing.

MOIRA:

Concede the pain. I, like you, concede
The pain of growing and the jagged ache
Denial gnaws upon his ragabone heart.
And yet I say this boy,
Knowing all that, will soon be blessed with joy,
For I shall bless him:

May your dumb five wits feel,
Your five wise senses know,
All life, all death reveal
One Word. Who calls this true?
The Parsee in the Fire,
The Hunted in the Grove—
Their wisdom, their desire
Its verity avow.
The cradled infant dreams
In the unity of their sight,
In the sleeping lover teems
Their intellectual delight,
The Dying Hero's might
From loss their Word redeems:
Read the hieroglyph aright,
All tongues together choir
The syllables of Love.

MORTA:

> That's noble, sister, but I'll spell you down.
> That mother's-milk and love-making routine
> With the ever-fashionable sacrifice
> To make the last act holy is a dream.
> Aren't you the sentimentalist! This boy is
> Fated to be handled by realities.
> I've got a tune for his condition. Here's
> A lullaby—

>> Lully, lullay.
>> You'll sleep, and sleep
>> And wake, and weep.
>> You'll take, to seek
>> Simplicity,
>> The lodestar of
>> Felicity,
>> But dreams will prove
>> Truth self-divides.
>> Lullay, lully,
>> Multiplicity
>> Taunts, derides
>> The simple soul
>> That seeks the Whole.
>> You'll sleep and sleep
>> Nor mind may rest
>> That I have blessed.

>> Bye, bye, bye,
>> Now that you lie
>> Under a Heaven
>> That's soiled and riven
>> By too many moons,

All bolts that threaten
Impiety
Are boons self-given
To men who've beaten
Ploughshares and hearts
In the natural way.
What reason fashions
By generous law
Your anarch passions
Will rend and gnaw
While affection's arts
In cold thought decay.
Lully, lullay.

FATHER:

To these blessings I will add my blessing:

I'll bless you, Son, with all the might our mortal
Franchise makes us heir to. The immortal

Possibility, the healing Whole,
Your Spirits offered to your hungering soul,

Your Norn, the incubus: Three most ripe fruits,
Heedless of thorns that stem all Absolutes.

The fruit I proffer's tougher: the protean splendor
Of mortal possibility, bestowing,

In the sacramental urgency of growing,
Hallows on its constant apprehender.

Accessible to pain's finality,
To unclad selfhood's meteoric claw,

Imagination's prodigality
An orbit past finality can draw

To trace the trials of mortal joy. The power
That transubstantiates your days

Of hived disorder that in Nature swarms
Be all my benison: All your assays

In passion find, and shape in thought, the forms
Of love and the anatomies of praise.

My voice woke up the baby and he cried.
His mother gave him suck. He slept content,
A minuscule of manhood. The fontanelle
Pulsed under his fuzz, moving a little.

A YEAR IN DIJON

Saint-Apollinaire.

September sunlight,
apples in the baskets,
potatoes in the bins,
rabbits in the barn,
cordwood under the outside stairs,
a tile-topped chimney lisping woodsmoke
pungent in the evening air,
odor of apples seeping through the floorboards,
nightlong dried-earth smell of the potatoes,
furtive skitters in the darkness,
mousefeet in the bins,
mice along the rafters,
snug in the farmhouse,
live coals in the grate the whole night long.
Dew stiffens gelid grass leaves.
Steps crunch the pebbly path
bringing bread in the morning,
morning bread
to Saint-Apollinaire.
We push dark shutters outward.
Their rims dazzle in lightfalls pouring
over the windowsill in splashes
awash on the scrubbed tiles.
The children in their smocks are singing
their schoolward way among the asters.

Dijon

In November they pollarded the plane trees,
    bound the branches into besoms,
        stacked faggots
to dry through half the winter by the wall.

Our Katy cried to see those amputees
    bear wintry rime on clumps of stumps
        like veterans of wars,
undecorated files at crooked rest.

The empty-sleeve men, one on a leg of pole,
    hump their way among the plane trees
        in crooked ranks
as Maquis infiltrate the guarded flanks

of courts, and vanish in a clank of grates
    to warm the marrow of their wounds
        at hissing hearths
where lopped branches redly singe and sigh.

When woodsmoke lifts from the Place de la République
    and air between the walls grows clearer
        the lined trees,
rainwashed familiars of paucity, remain,

Their knobs aswell with nodes of summer's verdure
    as though time and the sun could nurture
        and eke a future
of live limbs tousling the wind from every suture.

Vezelay

Preach me no preachments John Ruskin
of the Aspiration of pointed Arches,
of the "wing'd nobility" of buttresses.
I have voyaged over waters for the laving of my sight.
I have found a still font
where, in the amber twilight
from column to column the arches
leap, and the light hallows
the curvature of hollows
the rhythm of the columns
the anthems of the silence
ethereal masses. Heaven's
obsidian light pours down
on the joyous Doomsday
of Christ and the creatures
the zodiac of vintners
the sacrifice of oxen
the dogheaded devils
peoples of the earth.
Our sins upon the capitals
breathe in rippling light,
move in the fluent light,
move in their own commission
till in the mind this moment
turns stone,
stone in the mind carved
with devildogs and virgins
butchering the ox in
stone relief, the drunken
vintners in the mind's eye
stony-eyed, the creatures
of the mind arrested,

gargoyle imagination's
personae held in stone
carven on the capitals
under rippling vaultribs
dancing down the arches.
Each in the absolute
joy of strict proportion
leaps from stone to stone
image of the earthfolk,
image of this moment
carved in the mind,
all dooms dancing
toward that stone Resurrection:
Breath on the Tympanum.

1956

That week the fall was opulent. Vendanges,
　　Dancing, sunlight, autumn warmth, full larder
　　Before the endurable oncome of the winter.

Needing a haircut, I asked the coiffeur again
　　To cut it short. He shrugged, but, being genial,
　　Complied. A Samson came in for his marcel.

Musique à la radio cut short. Shrill voice:
　　Our fleet en route to liberate Suez!
　　Nasser, beware! Victory in two days!

Then glory used up all the largest type fonts
　　As Napoleonic ghosts in parachutes
　　Converged canalward on those camel-troops.

Coiffeur and Samson were ready for the glory.
　　But Egyptians, seeing Israel's guns, skedaddled
　　Before the Indo-China vets embattled

Them. The RAF pounded the desert
　　For two days. Meanwhile John Foster Dulles
　　(My countryman) put through long-distance calls

To God again, and passed the Moral Law
　　Again. Texas and Oklahoma cheered
　　His oil on troubled waters. It appeared

OK to Moscow too. Peace took the UN
　　By unsurprise. Beaten yet once again,
　　Dienbienphu yet unavenged, Pétain

Yet unavenged, Verdun. . . . My hair grew longer.
　　I went to the coiffeur again. This day
　　In short supply I found l'amitié.

I spoke of soccer, not Suez, nor glory.
　　His shears yet jabbed my head most dangerously.
　　The next man up read *Combat* sullenly.

L'amitié is scarce. A run on soap.
　　Hoarders have got the rice. There's no coal
　　In the coalyards. At the school, no oil;

What's plenty? A pyramid in the Magasin
　　Of canned-for-America grapefruit, tin on tin;
　　A sign says: PAMPLEMOUSSES ISRAËLIENS.

The ration of gas threatens the Cabinet.
　　Canal-boats on the Ouche fray weedy hausers.
　　Nobody mentions glory now, or the Gaza,

But curses the malign sphinx of history.
　　By the Arc de Triomphe they await who'll unriddle the past
　　And may, even now, be descending the mountain path.

A Letter to Wilbur Frohock

St-Apollinaire (Côte d'Or)
November, 1956

Cher Maître:

Neither my explication
of "Le Dernier Abencérage"
nor the almost-fluency
at quip and badinage

attested by your A-minus
a decade ago
in "Oral Intermediate
French" suffices now;

a beret is not enough.
Je puis acheter du pain
mais, when I go to the coalyard
as I do, again and again,

my first word or gesture's
carte d'identité,
sufficient proclamation:
"Je suis étranger."

"Sell you coal? My poor mother
Burns faggots in her mountain hovel—
You've la bombe atomique in your country—
Our children go barefoot in winter"

la marchande rails, distrait—
Besides, her coalyard's bare;
but, as you've said, the structure
—impeccable—of their

grammar reflects the logic
of the French mind. We've been here
two months. By now the neighbors
say "Bonjour, Monsieur";

in our village there are two eggs
for sale each second day,
reserved for the toothless aged
or a sick bébé

and when our boy got queasy
and couldn't take his meat
at l'épicerie they sold me
un oeuf for him to eat—

My accent's improving.

Gestures

Before train-time they swept across the track
Bare-headed or beretted, in a tide
    Bearing loaves
Of *pain d'épice,* bottles of Nuits-St-George
And Chambertin. The engine nudged a furrow
Across their crest and chuffled to a stop.
    They thrust the loaves and bottles

Of the best they had to give toward open windows
Where, bleared and grizzled, the late triumphant hosts
    Of Budapest
Outstretched their hands in pauperage and pain
And pride. *Vive la liberté! Vive
La liberté!* chanted the crowd. The few
    With French enough replied

"Merci" for Dijon's gifts of gratitude,
Of homage to their hopeless hope, of guilt
    That other died,
That other fought and fled, their futures left
Behind, that boy propped on a hard-backed bench,
A swollen bullet in his throbbing arm,
    While we communed with *pain*

D'épice and *premiers crus.* The engine, watered,
Whooshed and strained. The stock began to roll
    Toward the mountains:
A disused camp for Prisoners of War
Would roof them in while squat Red tanks patrol
All homeward roads past Austria. Then peace
    Settled from grimy skies

As a wild gull, daubed in coaltar, flounders
Disconsolately down to a joyless rock.
    In bitter weather
We heard that some escaped Hungarians,
One with a sling, from Dole toiled up the Juras
Toward the immaculate freedom of that zone
    That looms in Alpine snow.

Mi-Carême

We were surprised by Mi-Carême's obtruding
On half the acerb season, when the fishes'
Trials of frailty almost seemed habitual.
A small renunciation of the flesh is
A thorn, though not in truth a crown, until
What's done without no longer pricks regret.
Well, on the rue de la Liberté that day
The breeches' bulge, the gaygrin becks all told
In winks of mask what fireworks stuttered out:
The frivolous feast has come, beneath the gaze
Of Jacquemaire, who, steeple-tall, emerged
At the booming sennet of his hourly bells.
Such images as these helped to dispel
Almost all trace of Lenten abnegation
In resurrections of the corpse interred
At Mardi Gras:
                        Those monsters at Chalon
Had made incomparable mirth. Some strode
On longlegs teetering past the crowded eaves;
A pair of osier giants, heads like eggs
The last roc laid before the earth grew cool,
In couthless courtship dipped and ducked and danced,
Joy's colossi, rathe for ridicule,
Tunes tattered the air festooned with flags then
As instrumental joculators wove
In sinuous undulations in between
His lumbering ankles and the porte-cochère
That a nest of pulleys held in her skirts aloft.
Now green snow fell, turned paper in our hair
As La Reine des Roses in her sheen negligée
Floated on a swan afloat on streams
Of streamers, bobbing heads and foams of sound.

Then fezzed trombonist, houri tambourine,
Libidinous flügelhorn and urgent drum
Conducted outward all these orotund
And liberal-featured figments of our glee
Beyond the turret-portals of the city
With peals of jubilation, casting them
To exile in a wilderness of marshes.
On tabletops, from our café, we leaned toward
Their unabated pantomime, their sway
To inaudible rhythms as the wind returned
An intermittent summons from the river.
There, across the high bridge to the island
A grave tribunal of the bishopric
Attended, palled in funeral pomp, and poised
To cinder all that gaiety in the end.

At Mi-Carême they dance before me still,
Made midget by the distance, silhouettes
Moving mirrored over the sheen of Saône,
Their procreant gestures ravelling sky and water
With earth till purification of the flame.
Now false-faced gamins shake their clipper-clappers
Against the Lenten rectitude, remembering
The boil of blood, the surge of seed, the sensual
Plenitude before the human legend
Recalls us to supernal imitation
And the weights of sorrow under the haloed sun.

Fontaine-les-Dijon Revisited

How could we sleep in that pension
At the foot of the hill
Below the chapel
At Fontaine-les-Dijon?

There the carillon
Shattered the stained-
Glass silence
Of our sleep.

On this high hill
Where St. Bénigne was born
A monk in the Middle Ages
Clanged a clapper all night long

Remembering how his mother
When her term had come
Hauled her big belly
To this hill's rocky dome

So her son could be birthed
Nearer heaven, so a church
In his name be erected,
His Sainthood perfected

—Speared by the Romans—
And now this spot
Is hallowed, we dare not
Give it over to demons

Who possess the underworld
And pinch us with their spells
Unless driven back under the world
By the clang of God's bells

Which is why, at 4:30 this morning
A monk in a cassock, to mark
Each quarter-hour in the dark,
Tolls anthems fourteen minutes long

And we arise to meagre rations
Under a holy hill
Irascible as demons
Whose sleepless bed is in hell.

At the Roman Wall

After my classes at the Faculté
I join the lonely Fulbrights. Their café
Across Rue Chabot-Charny's an oasis
In a desert of impassive faces,
An island echoing in a heedless sea.
They huddle, and their tabled ground rejoices
To the flat yammer of their American voices.
They make each other homesick, and make me.

Here in this foreign one-horse town we're far
From convivial comforts of the familiar;
It's strange, missing the reassurance latent
In mere recognition, even the blatant
Blandness of a hometown storefront street,
Here, change in the pocket's no assurance.
Taste of the bread may seem an exile's durance
And dripping beeves make one distrust one's meat.

On this café wall a plaque of bronze
Announces that these very stones were once
The Castrum Romanum's perimeter,
Marking civilization's limit, or
Were plinths for Caesar's routs beyond Dijon
(Divio, then), when this carafe's deep vintage
Was guzzled here and paid for in a mintage
Judas might have clapped his palm upon.

Here, when howling helmed Burgundians swept
Against Castrum Divionense and leapt
These battlements, the stupored Roman legions
Hightailed south toward less anarchic regions
But left their temples, stocked with gods, behind.
Here, in the shade of ruined colonial splendor

Venus' charms were hawked by the one-eyed vendor
Whose amulets for Apollo cured the blind.

Here, Saint Bénigne stumbled, speared, in chains,
His mortal heart already in high heaven,
In triumph playing Christ's agon again.
Here pilgrims trod to touch his quick remains.
Here that good Catholic Chabot-Charny scorned
An evil queen and bull of Richelieu's,
Spared Huguenots for Saint Bartholomew's
And Jesus' sakes, whose Mercy they suborned.

See, on the Place du Théatre, Rameau stands
Statue-still, who, when he waved his hands,
Brought from the lutanists' and flautists' fingers
And their breath a counterpoint that lingers
Though peruqued ladies who to his gavottes
Turned on the arms of their pomaded lovers
Like moons 'round silver planets, beneath their covers
Of weary stone sleep next the sansculottes.

Here, I drink *vin ordinaire*. The grey
Twilight throbs with old wounds. I obey
Some homing instinct, and I think of places
Where the walls change like the ever-changing faces
In a boomtown crowd, once comforting to me.
There, unbounded by old stones, our choices
Seemed self-given, and selves, like our green voices
Unresonant with echoes, sounded free.

BROKEN LAWS

1

Under flat stones beside the creek
In their damp small lairs
The newts are biding
Their time,

Clenched fronds
Thrust uncurling
Through the dead leafmould

And the creek burbles
Louder than it has all winter,
Burbles with snow-melt and the run-off
After three days of rain.

The wind wrinkles now
With near-forgotten odors.
Something is about to happen.

Even those who've never seen it before
Know what to do.

2

Among the bedsprings,
Rusted cans,
Cardboard boxes pulped by rain

Settling on the raw dirt beside
Old bottles rags torn newspapers
And a headless rubber doll

The daisies cluster in the sun

Nodding or swaying as the wind sways
And the wide gaze of their yellow stare
Ringed with white rays
Fixes the center of the scene.

3

Waiting for the stones to ripen

The sun will lean
Down to touch the day
That lets us in

On what I am sent
Here to do

4

Looking up I see
That in the moon's absence
Once again

The stars
Are defining themselves
By their own lights.

They have been doing
This for a long time.

Any questions
Of identity

Or intention
Or the purpose of it all

Will have to be referred
To me.

    5

It is so still you
Hear the crinkle of the stars
Beneath the Milky Way switch
OFF/ON. OFF/ON. Nothing
Wrinkles the silence, only
Noise of light

Incalculable millions
Of stars   of years away

Until the sharp-
Smelling vixen's bark
Breaks over the huddled
Boulders, answered
By a wilder yowl or
Echo from the hill—

Questions of the cosmos are displaced by this.
In which burrow crouches the next meal?

    6

The man in the summer
Cottage down the road is
Dying.
It's cancer. He's

Aged a dozen years
Since last year. Still,
On brisk days he'll wear
His jaunty sweater

With the embroidered badge
That spells "Admiral."
His wife is the one
Now who drives

The car—at the Yacht
Club they say it will
Be a miracle
If he survives

Till Fall and how can he spend
The summer here, as though
The next breath of wind might not
Be the end?

7

Suppose that at the end of it
You recognize in
A thunderclap
Or a spark gap
What it was

That brought you to that end
What it is that out
Of the tedium of your doubt
You must affirm and bend
Your restless will to

What a time to amend
Your meandering along the rows
Of days like bushes bent
With blueberries or spined
With your basket nearly empty still to find

This is no mere
Berry feast or picnic where
The deer trampled the grass
Or where hungry you slept
On bare ground you kept

On the necessary way not
Observing the celebrations
Of the stations
You were sent to or what image
Devised all that you do

8

When the water holds so still
That every cloud
Boat and island shimmers upright in
Images of those
Sails clouds bluffs now seen as
Perfect in the sea

—A day with no circumference
Hung like the sound
Rung from a bell of light no motion save
The squall of gulls
In the only circles over
Islands far away

An exhalation of eternity
Desiring nothing—
We startle from this trussed in time
A sack of skin
Drawn over breath enough to last from our
First gulp to dying day.

9

Tonight a skein of wild geese
Churns the fading air.
With broken cries

The clattering wedge of their huge wings
Splits the sky
Rushing onward, followed by

The laggard few
Who heed exultant summons
Of that harsh cortège—

Breasting a wind that thickens,
Darker, they batter their way.
These

Could not hang back
At that call
But leapt

Finding at last their
Longed-for freedom, leaving
Everything for this.

10

Watching, listening
To the flight
Of the wind, the seasons

Of the night,
We stand astonished once again
By the grandeur of the world

Outside ourselves, our eyes
Enclosing at a glance
The flocks' mysterious return

And the falling
Stars among the stars that hold
Perpetual places on our mythic charts

Of monsters, queens, and murderers
Of monsters—or are those bold
Points the rusted holes

Made by spots of purer dew
Than any we shall walk upon
Piercing the sooty kettle of the sky

So that original light
Pours through in flecks like stars
Toward which we hurtle in our flight?

11

Not likely there, though,
The fulfillment of desire
Promised in

Commandments spelt
On the black basalt
Tables of our nights,

Inscribed on limestone days.
Their invocation says,
"THOU SHALT . . ."

We seek them by what light
Slips through the panes
Of dream windows

Wavering
While the moon in her own image
Creates the changed world anew

Then melts as dew
Dries at the coming
Of another light

Blazing
Across our bed,
Our breakfast table,

Coloring our walls, our lawns,
The busy schedule our fading
Dreams bequeath,

The broken laws
Almost deciphered on
This air we breathe.

ACKNOWLEDGMENTS

Three of the narratives are presented here for the first time: "The Love-Child," "Jane Doe," and "Samaritans." The others were published in journals whose editors I thank for their hospitality: "Buddies"in *Pequod* (1992); "A Barn Built in Ohio" in *Ontario Review* (1986); and "Shocks" in *The Hudson Review* (2005).

"Blessings," part I, is from *An Armada of Thirty Whales* (1954), there titled "Ode"; part II, from *A Little Geste and Other Poems* (1960), there titled "The Blessings." "A Year in Dijon" is from *The City of Satisfactions* (1963) except for "Fontaine-les-Dijon Revisited" and "At the Roman Wall," from *Hang-Gliding from Helicon* (1988). "Broken Laws" is from the collection so titled (1970).

Daniel Hoffman served as Poet Laureate in 1973–74, the appoint-
ment then known as Consultant in Poetry of The Library of Con-
gress. His first book, *An Armada of Thirty Whales,* was W. H. Auden's
choice for the Yale Series of Younger Poets Award in 1954. Among
his dozen subsequent volumes are *Brotherly Love,* a finalist in 1981
for both the National Book Award and the National Book Critics
Circle Award; *Beyond Silence:*   *2003;*
and *Makes You Stop and Think:*   of his
critical studies are *Faulkner's C*   tional
Book Award finalist, *Poe Poe*   es in
Swarthmore, Pennsylvania, and